**MASTER THIS!**

Gymnastics

Tracey Royle

WAYLAND

Printed by Wayland in 2012.

Hachette Children's Books
338 Euston Road
London NW1 3BH

Wayland Australia
Level 17/207 Kent Street
Sydney NSW 2000

All rights reserved.

Commissioning editor: Jennifer Sanderson
Senior editor: Claire Shanahan
Produced by Tall Tree Ltd
Editor, Tall Tree: Jon Richards
Designer: Ed Simkins

British Library Cataloguing in Publication Data
Royle, Tracey.
  Gymnastics. -- (Master this)
  1. Gymnastics--Juvenile literature.
  I. Title II. Series
  796.4'42-dc22

ISBN: 9780750268202

First published in 2009 by Wayland
Copyright © Wayland 2009
This paperback edition printed by Wayland in 2012

Printed in China

Wayland is a division of Hachette Children's Books,
an Hachette UK company.
www.hachette.co.uk

Picture credits
All photographs taken by Michael Wicks, except:
t-top, b-bottom, l-left, r-right, c-centre
Cover Dreamstime.com/Julia Taranova,
4 Dreamstime.com/Grosremy, 5 Dreamstime.com/Valeria
Cantone, 13t Jamie Lantzy, 14t Wally McNamee/Corbis
14b Dreamstime.com/Shariff Che' Lah, 17t Wally
McNamee/Corbis, 27t Frank May/epa/Corbis,
29l Dreamstime.com/Grosremy

The website addresses (URLs) included in this book were
valid at the time of going to press. However, because of
the nature of the Internet, it is possible that some
addresses may have changed, or sites may have changed
or closed down since publication. While the author and
publisher regret any inconvenience this may cause the
readers, no responsibility for any such changes can be
accepted by either the author or the publisher.

Disclaimer
In preparation of this book, all due care has been
exercised with regard to the advice, activities and
techniques depicted. The publishers regret that they can
accept no liability for any loss or injury sustained. When
learning a new sport it is important to get expert tuition
and to follow a manufacturer's instructions.

Acknowledgements
The author and publisher would like to thank the
following for their help and participation in this book:
Marriotts Gymnastics Club, Sophie Cripps,
Daniel Gardner, Jack Maydom, Mollie Smith
and Lauren Doherty

Contents

In the gym

Gymnastics is an exciting sport that combines agility, strength and timing to create breathtaking displays on various pieces of equipment, such as the floor, beam and vault.

Early gymnastics

People have been performing gymnastic exercises for thousands of years. The earliest male gymnasts performed naked, while women were banned from taking part. Gymnastics appeared at the Olympic Games in Athens in 1896. Rhythmic gymnastics (see pages 14–15) was first recognised in 1962 and appeared at the Olympics for the first time in 1996.

Diet

Gymnasts need to stay fit and healthy to perform at their peak. Eating the right foods is vital to keeping their bodies in shape. A healthy diet should include plenty of fresh fruit and vegetables and be low in fat. It should also have foods that contain lots of protein, such as chicken and beans, to help build muscles, and carbohydrates, such as pasta, to give you energy.

This gymnast is performing on a piece of apparatus called a pommel. His routine includes swinging his legs and body around the pommel, while holding onto the handles in the middle.

This gymnast is carrying out a routine on the asymmetric bars. She will perform swings, *leaps* and **somersaults** from one bar to the other.

Taking part

Gymnastics requires a great deal of physical fitness, but it can still be performed by men and women from very early ages (in some cases, before a child can walk) to the age of 70 and older.

However, not all of the disciplines are performed by everyone. Men and women perform on the floor and the vault, while only women perform on the beam and the asymmetric bars. Men perform on the pommel horse, the rings, the **parallel** bars and the high bar.

 # Clothing and kit

Clothing for gymnasts is quite simple. It should be close-fitting so that it does not get in the way, but not so tight that it restricts your movement. Other personal equipment includes hand grips and chalk.

What to wear

Girls train in **leotards** and occasionally gym shorts, while boys wear a leotard or a T-shirt and shorts. In competition, girls wear a leotard with either long or short sleeves. For rhythmic gymnastics (see pages 14–15), the leotards can be decorated with diamanté and sequins. Boys wear a leotard and shorts during competition floor exercises and the vault. They wear long trousers with stirrups (hoops at the bottom of each leg to go around the feet) and socks when competing on the other apparatus.

leotard and shorts

leotard and long trousers

leotard

Grips and chalk

Gymnasts wear hand grips during displays on the bars and rings. These are not compulsory, but they prevent the hands from ripping or tearing, which can occur during many hours of training. Men's hand grips are different from women's as men hold the bars and rings differently. Both men's and women's hand grips are caked in chalk (magnesium) using water or a spray.

Hand grips

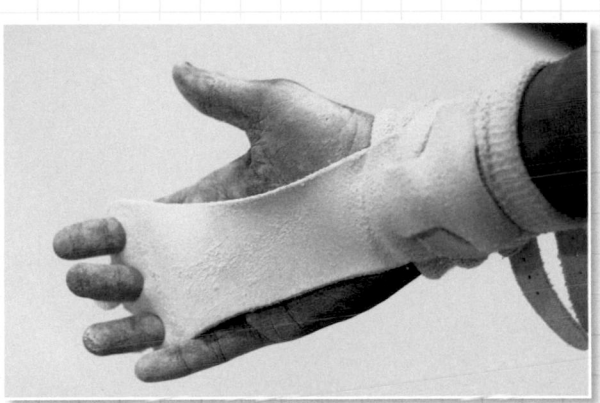

A man's hand grip has three finger holes to hook over the middle three fingers.

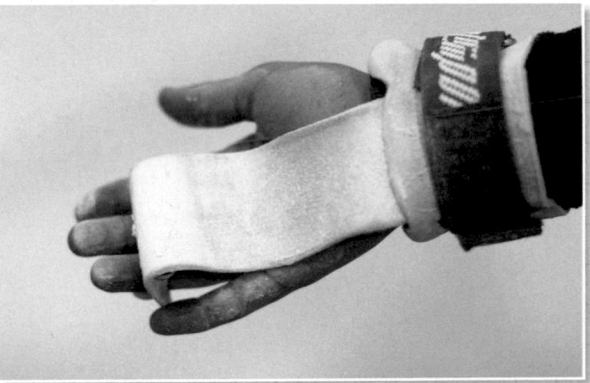

A woman's hand grip has two finger holes and is thinner than a man's. Young male gymnasts sometimes use these grips.

Chalking up

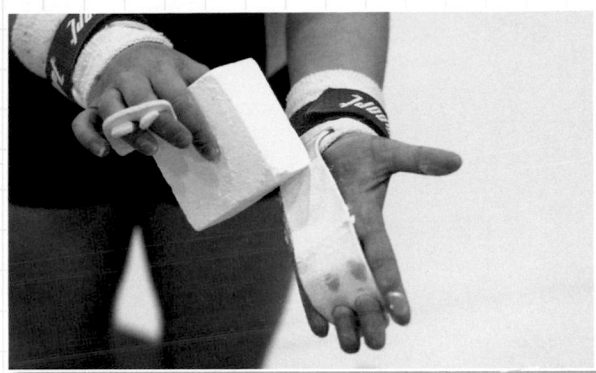

Solid blocks of chalk are rubbed onto hand grips to cover them.

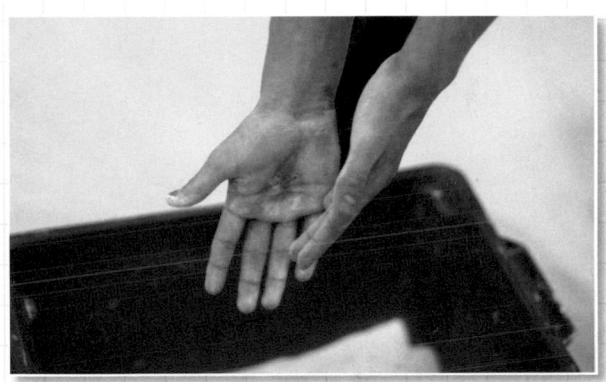

Loose chalk powder is rubbed onto the hands when hand grips are not used.

Top tip

You should never wear jewellery while doing gymnastics. Not only is it dangerous, but you will also be penalised if you wear jewellery during a competition. You should always tie back your hair so that it is not in your eyes.

 # Shapes and conditioning

Gymnastics is a very active sport and you should make sure that you are physically fit enough to take part. Your coach can show you several positions, called 'shapes', and exercises to improve your fitness.

Gymnastic shapes

Different shapes will help you train for different disciplines. You should concentrate on getting the positions correct and holding them for several seconds. Doing this will exercise specific muscles and improve your technique for different disciplines.

The arch is good at developing swinging and **tumbling** techniques.

The back support helps to develop body posture for parallel bars and the pommel.

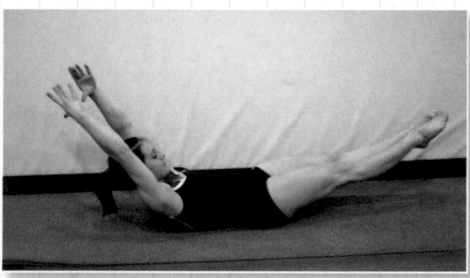

The dish helps to improve strength and techniques for swings and tumbles.

The front support is helpful for improving skills for the parallel bars and the pommel.

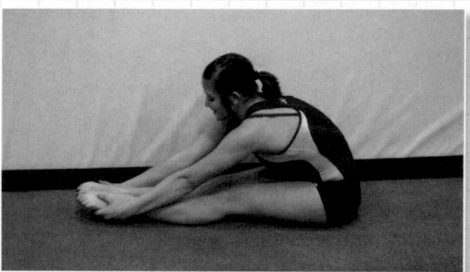

The **pike** shape is important for rotational, or turning, skills used in vaulting.

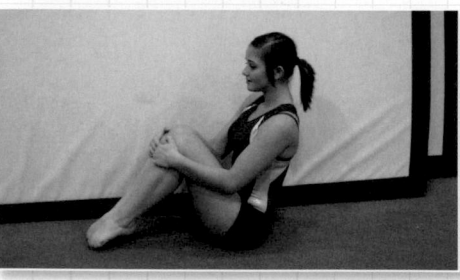

The tuck is helpful in developing tumbling skills.

Conditioning exercises

As well as shapes, there are several active exercises that can be used to improve technique and strength even further. These should be attempted only after the shapes have been mastered. For example, press-ups are taught after the basic front support shape has been perfected.

Press-ups

Basic press-ups are performed with the elbows held in. The gymnast lowers herself slowly until her nose touches the floor and then pushes herself up.

For an advanced press-up, the legs are lifted until the gymnast is pushing up from a **handstand** position. This develops arm and shoulder strength.

Sit-ups

Basic sit-ups (left) are performed with the feet under a wall bar before they are taken to an advanced level (see below).

This gymnast is performing an advanced sit-up. He has hooked his feet under the handle of a pommel and is carrying out sit-ups off the side.

 # The floor

The floor features some of the most breathtaking gymnastic performances, where male and female gymnasts demonstrate power, strength and grace in a series of simple moves and complicated tumbles.

Top tip

You can learn rolls correctly by performing them on a padded slope. This will make turning easier, allowing you to concentrate on getting the right technique.

Basic skills

The first floor skills learned are rolls, which can be forwards, backwards or sideways. Once basic rolls have been mastered, they can be developed into more advanced skills, such as handstand forwards rolls, **dive rolls** and somersaults.

The handstand is another important floor skill and it can also be used for other apparatus, such as the bars, beam and vault. The last important skill is the **cartwheel**, which is developed when learning how to tumble.

Forwards roll

1. The gymnast starts in a squat with her arms held out in front of her.

2. She puts her hands on the floor and rolls onto her back.

3. She lands on the balls of her feet and pushes herself upright.

In or out?

The edge of the floor is marked by a thick border – gymnasts cannot touch or go outside this border during a routine, otherwise they will be penalised.

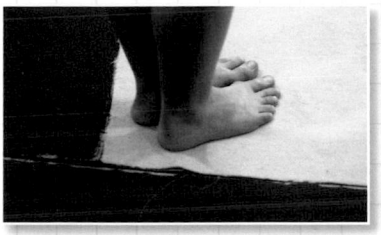
in

out

Floor competition

Both males and females compete on the floor. Females perform a routine lasting no more than 90 seconds, while men have a maximum of 70 seconds. These routines should contain tumbles, leaps, spins and jumps. Females' routines are performed to music.

This gymnast is performing a cartwheel. She keeps her legs wide apart to complete the move as smoothly as possible.

Straddle press to handstand

1

The gymnast places his feet wide apart and leans forwards.

2

He puts his hands shoulder width apart and raises his legs.

3

He brings his legs together to form a handstand.

Acrobatic gymnastics

Acrobatic gymnastics, or acro, takes place on the floor and combines elements of **artistic gymnastics** and acrobatics. Both men and women perform acrobatic routines. It involves groups of two to four gymnasts.

Working together

Acrobatic gymnasts have to trust their team-mates completely as they perform complicated balancing routines. There are five types of acrobatic gymnastics events: women's pairs, men's pairs, women's groups, men's groups and mixed pairs.

Two gymnasts perform a pair balance. When three gymnasts perform a hold it is called a trio balance (see page 13).

Pair balance

1 Gymnast 1 squats down and takes hold of gymnast 2. Gymnast 2 steps back onto gymnast 1's knee.

2 Gymnast 2 then steps back with her other foot, maintaining balance all the time.

3 With gymnast 1 carrying the weight of both gymnasts, gymnast 2 extends her arms to finish the balance.

The routines

Acro routines must contain throws, catches, tumbles, dances, balances and synchronised skills, where gymnasts perform the same move at the same time. Acrobatic gymnastics is performed on the same 12-metre-wide floor layout as artistic gymnastics. The floor is sprung to help the gymnasts to tumble in **unison**. Each routine is set to music and should last between two-and-a-half and three minutes.

Trio balance

Gymnast 1 steps back and out to one side so that her legs form a step up onto which gymnast 2 can climb.

Gymnast 2 climbs onto gymnast 1 until she is standing on her shoulders.

Gymnast 1 keeps her legs wide apart to maintain balance, while gymnast 2 stretches up her arms.

Gymnast 3 then climbs onto the back of gymnast 1, holding onto her shoulders and extending her legs on either side of gymnast 1.

Rhythmic gymnastics

Rhythmic gymnastics is very elegant. It is performed on the floor and involves gymnasts using a variety of hand-held apparatus, such as clubs, balls, hoops and ribbons, to create a series of flowing movements.

Star file

NADIA COMANECI
The 'perfect' gymnast

Romanian Nadia Comaneci was the first gymnast to be awarded a perfect score of 10 for her display on the asymmetric bars at the 1976 Olympic Games. She went on to win five Olympic gold medals at the 1976 and 1980 Games. Today, she works as a television commentator and is Honorary President of the Romanian Gymnastics Federation and the Romanian Olympic committee.

Individuals and teams

Although it is more common for women and girls to perform rhythmic routines, men are increasingly taking part. Performances involve individuals or groups of up to five gymnasts who work together, combining graceful jumps, balances and rolls while throwing, catching and twirling the apparatus.

A gymnast performs using the ribbon, twirling it to draw spirals, snakes and circles.

The apparatus

Rope
The rope is made from either **hemp** or an artificial material and has a knot at one end. The routine is performed with the rope folded or open and held in one or both hands.

Hoop
The hoop is made from wood or plastic and measures 80 to 90 centimetres across. Gymnasts move the hoop around and above them, while holding it with different parts of the body, such as their legs and feet.

Ball
The ball is made of rubber or a synthetic material. It measures between 18 and 20 centimetres across and has a minimum weight of 400 grams. The ball is the only piece of apparatus that is never gripped: it may only be balanced on a part of the body, rolled over or bounced. Ball routines show smooth movements between the ball and gymnast, with powerful throws and precise catches.

Clubs
The clubs are between 40 and 50 centimetres long and weigh around 150 grams each. Gymnasts must show club skills, such as circles and throws, as well as moves that combine these skills with body movements, such as leaps and somersaults.

Ribbon
The ribbon is at least 6 metres long. There is a stick that is 50 to 60 centimetres long at one end. Gymnasts use the ribbon to draw circles, spirals and snakes.

 # The beam

Performing on the beam requires great courage, as gymnasts tumble and leap on a beam that is 10 centimetres wide. Even so, these routines are some of the most graceful in gymnastics.

Long and thin

The beam is 1.25 metres high and 5 metres long. It is made of wood that is covered in a soft leather. Training beams are softer and have more spring than competition beams so that you can perform more repetitions and practise harder skills.

Spin

Raising her right leg, the gymnast lifts onto the toes of her left foot. She holds up her arms to help with her balance.

Pushing with the toes of her left foot, she spins around to face her original direction.

This gymnast is performing a leap on the beam. She has made a leg split, so that her legs are parallel to the beam.

Beam routines

Beam routines are created by gymnasts and their coaches and should last no longer than 90 seconds. These routines must include acrobatics, such as **walkovers**, and a series of leaps, one of which must include a 180-degree leg split, as well as spins, **mounts** and **dismounts**.

Gymnasts often practise difficult routines on 'low' beams. These are training beams that have the same dimensions as competition beams, but are set low to the ground to reduce the risk of injury.

Star file

OLGA KORBUT
Beam pioneer

Born in 1955, Olga Korbut became a star at the Olympics of 1972 and 1976, where she performed as part of the USSR (former Soviet Union) team. She was the first gymnast to perform a backwards somersault on the beam. In total, she won four Olympic gold medals and two silver medals.

Backwards walkover

Arching her back, the gymnast steps back onto one foot to start the walkover.

The gymnast places her hands on the beam, while her **momentum** carries her legs over.

Placing her right foot first, the gymnast continues to pull her body and left leg over.

With both feet placed on the beam, the gymnast brings her body upright to finish the walkover.

The vault

For the vault, male and female gymnasts sprint down a runway before bouncing off a springboard to perform twists and somersaults over a vaulting table. This discipline requires great power and accuracy.

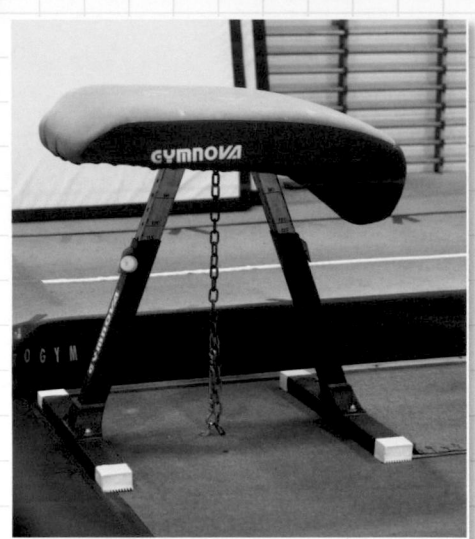

The padded vault table can be set to different heights – 1.25 metres for females and 1.35 metres for males. At the base of the vault is a springboard, which is a bouncy platform set on several springs. Jumping on the springboard allows gymnasts to spring higher.

A gymnast performs a handspring vault followed by a somersault. You need a powerful run-up, otherwise you will not get enough speed and height on your vault.

Different vaults

The handspring is the first vault that gymnasts learn. The three individual parts to this vault (the run-up, the flight on, and the flight off and landing) are taught separately. Once you have mastered all of these, the three parts are put together to perform the basic handspring and then developed into other vaults.

Handspring

After the springboard, the gymnast puts her hands on the vault.

Both legs come over together and she pushes off with her hands.

Her legs continue to come over to land firmly on the mat.

Competition vaults

In competition, there are five female vault groups, including the forwards handspring with twists, handspring into somersaults and Yurchenko vaults. The five male vault groups include direct, Yamashita and Tsukahara vaults. Yurchenko, Yamashita and Tsukahara vaults are named after the gymnasts who developed them.

Tsukahara vault

The gymnast turns sideways as he lands on the springboard.

He places his hands in line with the vault and brings his legs over in a cartwheel.

At the top of the cartwheel, the gymnast pushes off the vault and twists his body.

After pushing off, the gymnast performs a backwards somersault.

Asymmetric bars

During an asymmetric bars routine, female gymnasts swing around two bars, performing **circles**, twists and **releases**. The display should be graceful and flowing and without any pauses or falls during the routine.

The bars

The two bars run parallel to each other but they are set at different heights. The high bar is 2.45 metres off the ground and the low bar is 1.65 metres, with the distance between the bars ranging from 1.3 to 1.8 metres. If you are very tall, you may ask to have both bars raised during a competition.

This gymnast has just mounted the asymmetric bars using an upstart mount, also known as a kip, where she swings under the lower bar. Gymnasts usually mount the bars without help, but they can use a springboard if they want to mount directly onto the higher bar.

Swings and starts

Routines are up to 40 seconds long and should contain releases, circle skills around the bars and a dismount. If you fall, you must mount the bars within 30 seconds or the routine is ended.

Dismount

The gymnast tucks into a pike position during her final swing, to generate enough speed.

Backwards giant swing

The gymnast holds her body straight at the top of the swing.

On the downswing, she bends her body slightly.

She lets go of the bar, shoots her toes upwards, then arches her body.

The gymnast moves her legs apart to avoid the lower bar.

She brings her legs back together before the next swing.

Tucking her legs into her chest, she completes a front somersault and lands on both feet.

Parallel and high bars

These male disciplines are both performed on bars, but the skills required for them are very different. Performing on the high bar involves building swings into releases and **catches**, while the parallel bars involve swings, turns and twists between the bars.

The parallel bars

The gymnast has to mount the 2-metre-high parallel bars on his own, although he may use a springboard to do so. The two bars are between 42 centimetres and 52 centimetres apart and gymnasts use them to perform routines that include handstands, somersaults, turns and **holds**, before finally dismounting to one side.

Swing to handstand

1

The gymnast starts to bring his legs forwards.

2

He then begins to swing his legs back with enough force to lift his body behind him.

3

At the top of the swing, he needs to work hard to hold the handstand.

The high bar

The bar is made of metal and is 2.55 metres above the ground. The routines are similar to those performed on the asymmetric bars, and include swings, turns, somersaults, releases and dismounts. During training, these moves are practised over a large pit that is filled with foam to protect you should you fall.

This gymnast is being lifted onto the high bar by his coach at the start of a routine.

Giant swing with twist

The gymnast maintains a firm body position at the top of his swing.

At the bottom, he bends slightly so that his feet lead the upwards swing.

To perform a twist, the gymnast lets go with one hand at the top of a swing. He spins his body around 180 degrees to face in the opposite direction. He changes from a forwards to a reverse grip.

Top tip

Your training routine should include the dish and arch shapes (see pages 8–9). These are helpful in conditioning your body and perfecting the techniques needed to perform swings on both the parallel and high bars.

The rings

This piece of apparatus shows the strength, flexibility and control of male gymnasts as they perform acrobatic swings and powerful holds while suspended 2.75 metres above the floor.

wooden dowel

The hand grips used on the rings have pieces of dowel, or small wooden rods, in them. These rods are inserted into loops in the hand grips just under the tips of the fingers. As the gymnast's fingers wrap around the rings, these dowels help him to grip the rings.

Holds

To perform a hold well, the gymnast needs to be stationary for a number of seconds. The L hold sees the gymnast's body and legs form an 'L' shape. For the iron cross, the gymnast holds his arms out straight to the sides at shoulder height while suspending his body. This is a difficult move and requires a lot of upper body strength. In the Maltese cross, the gymnast holds his body parallel to the floor at ring height.

This gymnast is performing an L hold. During a competition, he has to keep still in this hold for at least two seconds, otherwise he will be penalised.

Swings

The giant swings performed on the rings are similar to those performed on the high bar. The gymnast swings from one handstand to another with his arms extended. Other moves that are performed during a competition routine are a swing to a handstand, a dismount and a hold.

Top tip

During a routine, you should always look to keep the ropes holding the rings tight. If the ropes go slack at any point, you could be hurt as the rings will jar with each swing.

This gymnast is performing a dismount. He has built up enough momentum for him to perform a somersault after releasing the rings and then land on both feet.

Swing

On the upwards swing, the gymnast's body bends, so the feet are raised high.

Towards the top of the swing, the gymnast's body straightens out.

His body arches slightly during the downwards swing.

The pommel

Pommel is one of the hardest male gymnastic disciplines as it requires strength over the whole body. The arms and upper body have to support you, while the legs and stomach keep your body rigid during circles, **flares** and dismounts.

Getting on and off

As with the parallel bars, the gymnast mounts without any help. Dismounting is usually to a landing mat that is placed to one side.

Dimensions

The pommel is 1.15 metres high and 1.6 metres long. There are two handles in the middle, which the gymnast grips when performing.

Pommel is practised on a mushroom. This is closer to the ground than a pommel, so there is less chance of injury when practising moves such as flares.

The routine

Each routine should be continuous, without the gymnast stalling or falling off. It should include double leg circles, where the gymnast spins around the pommel with both legs held together, and flares, where the legs are wide apart during the spin. Also included are scissors, where the legs straddle either side of the pommel, and swings up to handstands.

Double leg circles

1. With both hands on the handles, the gymnast swings his legs together.

2. With his back straight, his legs are brought in front of his body.

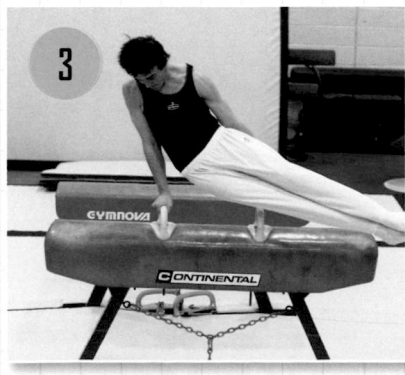

3. He raises his left hand and puts his weight on his right as his legs pass beneath.

4. The legs now pass behind the gymnast as he completes a full circle.

To perform a dismount, this gymnast has swung up into a handstand, before landing on both feet beside the pommel.

 Taking it further

Taking part in gymnastics can be very demanding and requires many hours of training. Your local club will be able to give you guidance and coaching to develop the skills you need.

Finding a club

Use the Internet to find a suitable gymnastics club near to where you live, and check out the websites of your local and national gymnastics organisations. Once you have joined a club, you will have the chance to enter competitions at different levels, from local to regional, and maybe even to international level.

Top tip

Check that the coaches at the gymnastics club you want to join have the correct qualifications. You can check these out by looking at the website of your national gymnastics organisation.

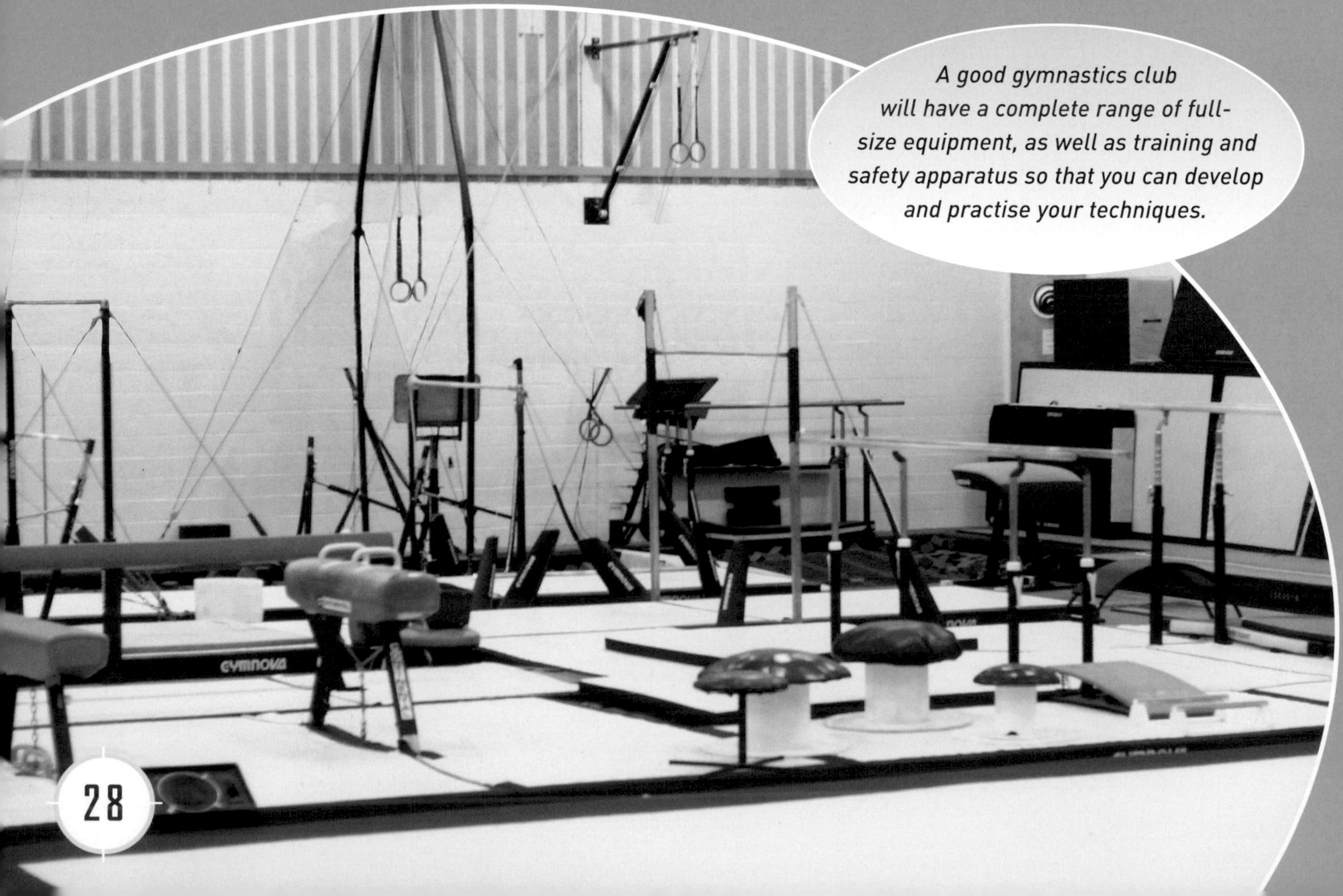

A good gymnastics club will have a complete range of full-size equipment, as well as training and safety apparatus so that you can develop and practise your techniques.

Competition

Gymnastic routines are overseen by a panel of judges that awards points to decide the winners. Gymnasts have a starting value of points, which is decided by the difficulty of techniques used in the routine. These starting points and the difficulty of various moves are laid out by the FIG (*Fédération Internationale de Gymnastique*), the organisation that oversees gymnastics around the world. Points are then deducted for mistakes made during the display, such as falls and stumbles.

Other gymnastic sports

Gymnastics techniques can be used in several sports, such as trampolining, which uses similar twists and somersaults. Diving also uses gymnastics skills, and many of the conditioning exercises, such as the pike (see pages 8–9), are used to teach the correct body positions during a dive.

A panel of judges studies a performance at the Men's European Team championships in 2008. At big competitions, such as the Olympics, there are nine judges for each piece of apparatus.

Glossary

artistic gymnastics gymnastics routines that are performed on various pieces of apparatus, such as the floor, the pommel and the bars.

cartwheel a move where gymnasts make a sideways spin of their whole body after putting their hands on the floor.

catches a move performed on the high bar and asymmetric bars where the gymnast catches hold of the bars, after letting go of them to perform another move in the air.

circles a move that sees the gymnast move his or her whole body in a circle around a piece of apparatus. Circles are performed on the parallel bars and the pommel.

dismounts a move where the gymnast lands with his or her feet on the floor after performing on a piece of apparatus, such as the beam, vault, bars, rings or pommel.

dive rolls when a gymnast jumps high in the air and then lands into a forwards roll.

flares a pommel move where the gymnast spins around with his legs wide open.

handstand a move where gymnasts lift their whole body off the floor while upside down.

hemp a plant with fibres that can be woven together to make hard-wearing cloth or rope.

holds a move where the gymnast remains still in a certain position for a number of seconds.

leaps moves where the gymnast jumps high into the air, taking off on one foot and landing on the other foot.

leotards tight-fitting outfits that cover the body from the shoulders to the tops of the legs.

momentum the combination of an object's weight and movement.

mounts the first skill in a routine performed on the beam, vault, bars, rings or pommel, when the gymnast gets onto the equipment.

parallel when two bars, or lines, are separated by an equal distance at every point.

pike a gymnastics position where the gymnast bends his or her body at the waist while keeping the legs straight.

releases a gymnastics move where the gymnast lets go of a piece of apparatus to perform another move, before catching hold of the apparatus again. Releases are performed on the high bar and the asymmetric bars.

somersaults moves where gymnasts spin head over heels in mid-air. Somersaults can be performed forwards and backwards.

tumbling acrobatic skills such as somersaults linked together along the floor, usually on a diagonal. Only the hands and the feet should touch the floor during a tumbling sequence.

unison when skills are performed at the same time by a group of gymnasts.

walkovers moves where gymnasts put their hands on the floor, lift their legs over their body, put their feet on the floor and stand upright.

Gymnastics organisations

There are many organisations around the world that oversee gymnastics at various levels, from regional up to international. Each discipline also has its own organisation giving specialist advice.

The FIG oversees gymnastics around the world, representing all disciplines, including artistic, rhythmic and trampoline.

British Gymnastics oversees gymnastics throughout the UK. It provides advice on courses, qualifications for coaching and finding your nearest gymnastics club.

The International Gymnastics Hall of Fame celebrates the sport's best athletes, as well as the others who have contributed to gymnastics, including coaches and judges.

Further reading

There are plenty of books available for the newcomer as well as the more experienced gymnast.

Know Your Sport: Gymnastics Gifford, Clive (Franklin Watts, 2008)
A Perfect 10 Higgins, Chris (Hodder Children's Books, 2008)

Websites

The Internet is a great place for information on techniques, advice and chatrooms where you can exchange training tips.

www.drillsandskills.com
A website with tips and advice on graded skills for each piece of apparatus.

www.tulsagymnastics.com
Contains advice for parents, coaches and gymnasts on training both in the gym and at home.

www.fig-gymnastics.com
The website of the FIG, which has the latest news from around the world and links for information on all aspects of gymnastics.

Index